# Down The Rabbit Hole

*Creative Talents Unleashed*

# GENERAL INFORMATION

## Down The Rabbit Hole

**By**

Creative Talents Unleashed

1st Edition: 2017

This Publishing is protected under Copyright Law as a "Collection". All rights for all submissions are retained by the Individual Author and or Artist. No part of this publishing may be Reproduced, Transferred in any manner without the prior **WRITTEN CONSENT** of the "Material Owner" or its Representative Creative Talents Unleashed.

*Creative Talents Unleashed*

www.ctupublishinggroup.com

**Publisher Information**
**1st Edition: Creative Talents Unleashed**
**info@ctupublishinggroup.com**

This Collection is protected under U.S. and International Copyright laws

Copyright © 2017: Creative Talents Unleashed

ISBN-13: 978-1-945791-33-8 (Creative Talents Unleashed)
ISBN-10: 1-945791-33-0

# Credits

## Book Cover
Raja Williams

## Creative Director
D.B. Hall

## Editors
Authors Responsible For Own Work

## Foreword
Lyne Beringer

# Foreword

*Tick tock says the magic clock*

*In a language that's part of the soul*

*Get in line for the gate*

*You don't want to be late*

*For your trip down the rabbit hole...*

Our everyday lives are filled to the brim with mostly ordinary things, like work, taking and picking up the dry cleaning, school, homework, dinner, and striving to have enough time for family and friends. We are busy in this modern world, filled with reality... and yet something is missing.

But what if you could sit down for just a little while and escape to someplace special....someplace magical and quirky? What if you could escape by slipping down the rabbit hole to a place of your choosing? What if you travel somewhere you've never been and be back before anybody even knew you were gone? What if reading the adventures of others inspired you to embark on some adventures of your own?

It gives me great pleasure to invite you inside the pages of this book. You will find all kinds of lovely people, places and things. You can meet Alice or Dorothy or the infamous Mr. Rabbit. You can slip easily down the rabbit hole and be transported to worlds that contain the ordinary and not so ordinary.

*"Down the Rabbit Hole"* is a collective work of writings from poets who like you, live their lives inundated with the challenges and demands of everyday life. They have unlocked the door to boundaries we all make for ourselves and turned those boundaries into fantastic, beautiful worlds to both help ease the boredom and perhaps spark the imagination.

Go ahead and make that cup of tea…add honey or sugar if you'd like…then sit down, close your eyes, and prepare to be transported to places you have never traveled to before. Come with me… I've got your hand. Here we go……. Down the Rabbit Hole.

*Lyne Beringer*, Author of "Alaskan Vogue - Poetry From the Land of Ice and Shadows"

# Table of Contents

Foreword   v

## Poets whisk us away to fantasy land

| | |
|---|---|
| Time<br>*D.B. Hall* | 2 |
| All Smiles – (Cheshire)<br>*Ann Christine Tabaka* | 3 |
| Cabbages and Kings<br>*Susan E. Birch* | 4 |
| Drink Me<br>*Tracy Seiden* | 8 |
| A Nonsense Adventure! (The Best Kind) Part 1<br>*Amrita Valan* | 9 |
| A Nonsense Adventure! (The Best Kind) Part 2<br>*Amrita Valan* | 11 |
| Unchained Alice<br>*Christa Frazee* | 13 |
| Ruby Slippers<br>*Maggie Mae* | 15 |
| Mad Hearted Crazy<br>*Jaqui Slade* | 16 |

# Table of Contents

The Wizard of Od     17
*Kelly Klein*

## Sprinkle magic words upon these pages poets

Winky Willy World     22
*Tammy S. Thomas*

A Cat's Early Morning Walk     23
*Shawn Chang*

My Blue Shoes     26
*Tammy S. Thomas*

A Wish in the Wings     27
*Justin R. Hart*

The Circus     29
*Ariana V. Cherry*

Wander Land     31
*Shelly Ambrose*

Wakeful Dreaming     32
*Valormore De Plume*

Peter Pan     33
*Bevan Boggenpoel*

# Table of Contents

Shades of Orange     34
*Steve Lay*

Wonderland     35
*Lyne Beringer*

Shhh! I'm Catching a Buzz!     36
*Peter V. Dugan*

## Taste the adventure that awaits

Rainbow Slide     38
*D.B. Hall*

Milk Chocolate Meltdown     39
*Elizabeth Daniel*

Mythical Magic     40
*Bevan Boggenpoel*

Chasing Rainbows While Stuck on Narcotics     41
(Prescription of course!)
*Ariana R. Cherry*

Haunted Solstice     43
*Peter V. Dugan*

Dorothy     44
*Jacqui Slade*

# Table of Contents

A Little Wicked — 46
*Mary Langer Thompson*

Rabbit Hole Poets — 47
*Hugh Dysart*

I Am Woman — 48
*Susan E. Birch*

Dorothy's Discovery — 49
*Tracy Seiden*

Cabbage Dreams — 50
*Lynn White*

## Let your words dance along golden pathways

Playing With Kings — 52
*Dale E Werner*

Punctuality is the Key — 54
*Elizabeth Daniel*

Sleepy Beauty — 55
*Shelly Ambrose*

Neverland — 56
*Kristi L. Phillips*

# Table of Contents

Rabbit Hole     57
*Kristi L. Phillips*

Like Alice     59
*Lynn White*

Home Sweet Home     60
*Christa Frazee*

Ruby Slippers     62
*Maggie Mae*

You Are Mad Dear Grandma     63
*Susan E. Birch*

Larry and the Fly     64
*Tammy S. Thomas*

Harvey     65
*Steve Lay*

## A place where words achieve goals created by dreams

A Ghostly Cold -Ode to the Flying Dutchman     68
*Ken Allan Dronsfield*

Wonderland     69
*Maggie Mae*

# Table of Contents

| | |
|---|---|
| From One Cirrus to Another<br>*Elizabeth Daniel* | 71 |
| Alice in Wonderland<br>*Bevan Boggenpoel* | 72 |
| Enchantment<br>*Shelly Ambrose* | 73 |
| Open Season<br>*Brenda-Lee Ranta* | 74 |
| Autumn's Ascending Spring<br>*Justin R. Hart* | 76 |
| Kitty Kisses<br>*Leila Samarrai* | 79 |
| Walk the Walk<br>*Maria Barba* | 81 |
| Unrestrained Dreams<br>*D.B. Hall* | 82 |

# Epilogue

| | |
|---|---|
| The Starving Artist Fund | 84 |
| CTU Connections | |

Poets whisk us away to fantasy land

# Time

Wait Mr. Rabbit
Please tell me
why are you late?

Oh dear!
Oh my!
Because you stopped me that is why.
Now I am here
and not there!
My clock has no time
It is your fault not mine!
Oh dear!
Oh my!
SHHHHSH
No No No
It is your fault for stopping me.
Now we are both late
quiet late
very late
quiet very late
and I am quite very confused
and I have no time for that!
Absolutely no time
Oh dear!
Oh my!
Look at the time!
Excuse me miss
I have to run
I am rather late.


D.B. Hall

# All Smiles – (Cheshire)

Hello, he said
With a toothy grin
Who are you?
And where have you been?

I looked all around
But all I could see
Were big glowing teeth
Smiling back at me

High up in the tree
He slowly appeared
From nose to tail
It was rather weird

He was striped orange
And utterly rotund
Hearing him laugh
Left me quite stunned

Then once again
He was gone in a flash
My head still confused
Away I did dash

Was that all real
Or an illusion I had
All that I know is
That cat was quite mad


*Ann Christine Tabaka*

# Cabbages and Kings

I sat beside a chuckling brook
Beneath the trees, a shady nook,
To browse a passage of my book.
The buzzing bees, the gentle breeze,
And heat of day soon overtook
And I began to drowse.
A nudge awoke me, there she stood
Looking as I thought she would
In pinafore of pristine white
Her eyes and dress cornflower bright
And reaching up a delicate hand
To settle the eponymous 'band'.
"If you won't take the time ..." said she
"We'll never get where we need to be".
And with a frown she then looked down
To where I had been dozing.
Pointing out the rabbit hole
On which I'd been reposing
and I....FELL

.......and landed with a certain flair
Upon a somewhat wobbly chair
Placed at a table fair and square.
"Oh do drop in..." the hatter smirked
".... and kindly take your ease. Have some tea
And sandwiches. Have anything you please".
"But tell me first, I beg you say..."
(and his tone now dripped with malice)
"...before we send you on your way,
WHAT HAVE YOU DONE WITH ALICE?"
"Cease this at once" said a gentle voice
"You know, when falling, we have no choice.
She smiled politely and daintily sat.

# Down The Rabbit Hole

"I've been" she said" to see the cat"
The Hatter asked what the cat had to say
"Oh the cat wasn't in, and I firmly refuse to
Converse with his grin, it's far too sane".
I thought this statement quite inane
just as I....FELL
.......And bounced upon a Tweedle who,
Without a bow or 'how do you do',
But with a somewhat purple face
Asked if I was in the race
As if people falling from the sky
Was 'everyday' and 'by the by'
I hadn't come for a caucus race
But jogged along to keep the pace.
Dum and Dee, right by my side,
Assured me I would soon be dried
From all the tears that Alice wept.
So, caucusing, we gaily stepped
Until "Race over!" the Dodo cried
And everyone looked behind with pride
To measure just how far they'd run
And calculate a circular sum.
'Award the prize' said the Lory to me
But at that moment, thankfully I ….FELL

...Into a dune quite deep and steep
Where perched the Carpenter to weep.
'Just let him be' the Walrus said
'And help me find an oyster bed!
Time to exercise again
Stretch the legs and air the brain! '
I stared at him suspiciously,
He raised an eyebrow back at me.

## Down The Rabbit Hole

I crossed my arms and shook my head
'You forget I've read the book ' I said
'To feed your greed you basely lied
And carried out molluscacide! '
The Carpenter sniffed and sobbed some more
The Walrus huffed and paced the shore.
'Twas only meant to be a snack
We truly meant to take them back
But they were so deliciously plump
A bit like you ' ...this made me jump
So that I....FELL

…And landed on a roof of thatch
Then slid onto a carrot patch.
The Rabbit cried out "Mary-Anne,
Bring out here my gloves and fan."
Oh-Oh, I thought, don't touch the 'shrooms
Or else I'll grow to fill the rooms.
The Rabbit fussed and checked the time,
Then, as his watch began to chime,
He shrieked "I am so very late!"
And ran out of the garden gate.
He quickly disappeared from view
Without goodbye or fond adieu
Just as I …..FELL

…And found myself in an easy chair
Beside a fire and aware of a glare
From an elderly gent clutching a book
Who, with a somewhat bewildered look,
Asked me what I was doing in his room
And please would I leave and make it soon!
I told of my journey and the fix I was in,

It was at this point he started to grin.
"I'm Charles Dodgeson he said and I wrote that book
For I went on that madcap journey you took.
I know how you feel for it almost drove me insane.
I fear my dear Alice has been meddling again.
Leave this to me, I will take Alice to task
But there is just one small thing I would ask.
Please, when you leave, don't fall through the floor
Just curtsy politely and leave by the door."

*Susan E Birch*

# Drink Me

So simple a request
So monumental the task
Brush aside your fears
Step inside
To follow you must be right in size
What world awaits
Past hesitation's gate
Drink me and investigate

So down it went
She standing tall
Shirk she did
Now she was small
Through the door
She followed once more
To what treasures
This new world had in store

*Tracy Seiden*

# A Nonsense Adventure! (The Best Kind) Part 1

Down the tricky rabbit hole
I descended an awful depth
The ground fell from under my feet
'twas a downward leap of faith.
Growing smaller and smaller
Somehow I grew taller, reaching heights unknown.
The door knob bumped against my head
And caused a swollen collar bone.
But I hit the floor at last, Thank God,
'twas made of checkered stones.
Through a giant keyhole I saw a world instead,
Opened up like an oyster, in its pretty shell.
The sky was crazy crimson
but the clouds were bleak and pale...
In the garden, The Duchess sat
(plonk upon a mad hatter's hat),
She was rather busy, spinning the tallest tale.

The Duchess she sat, upon the hat,
So madly glad and gay,
The March hare was quite certain
That 'twas the merry month of May!
The Red Queen would have none of it
So throwing a huffy puffy fit,
She cried out in a puffy huff,
"I don't see the point of it!"
Brandishing a sword as dull and dry
As her mindless wit,
"Off with their heads" she loudly shrieked,
"Now just get on with it!"
The undulating caterpillar
Shrugged a soft yet sinewy spine,

## Down The Rabbit Hole

It looked cuddly cute and strangely mute
Holding an ornate hookah fine.
The Cheshire cat appeared too for a little while
With an almost-but-not-quite, enigmatic smile.
I drank my tea out of a dainty lobster shell
'twas a lovely hollow scoop with a tiny pointy tail
Spiraling out of my fingers, wriggling very well
And in it swam, snarling, a sniveling snooty snail.
The tea was lovely, the tea was good
There were cakes and scones, and mouthwatering food,
But they didn't behave, the way good food should.
The cakes refused to allow the edgy knife
To carve out even the thinnest slice
Jumping off the table for their scrumptious lives.
'twas naughty of them, they were just not nice.
The scones were sadly falling apart, silently they cried
Dripping bitter butter from their moist and runny eyes
Limp with defeat they complained
how the walrus always lied.
I fell to wondering why they were so sad
I really couldn't eat the poor lads
So I sipped my lobster shell of tea
And asked the scones to tell me
Who the Walrus was and what was his crime
But that's a story for another time.

*Amrita Valan*

# A Nonsense Adventure! (The Best Kind) Part 2 - The Scones Tale

"The walrus said he was taking us
Only for a walk...
He said he packed us scones along
For a harmless little talk,
He even said we should enjoy a cuppa
He promised it would be smoking hot.
Sadly
A few things to mention
The walrus simply forgot.
How we would all be served for tea
In an elegant ceramic pot...
"The time has come!",
Said the walruses in whiskered unison
For a walk and a talk, and one on one
C'mon scones! Let's have some fun.
All the time they were groaking us,
Oh! What a cruel and heartless con.
My rabbit hole spread out far and wide
Thin at the poles bulging at the hips
It held an entire world all neatly curled
Like the smoky spirals from the caterpillar's lips.
The scones escaped, they performed back flips
With squishy jumps and crumbly leaps
The ants and spiders gobbled up quite a heap.
I didn't lose my head at this
For it was screwed real tightly on.
The rabbit hole grew narrower now
And rather steep and small.
My head swelling up much too fast for me to fit at all.
Finally I found an opening, and burst out
Like a plump nut from its crackling shell,
Rolling round and round, to the bottom of my garden wall.

## Down The Rabbit Hole

The garden spiders were not amused.
On their world wide web, I remain accused.
Of smashing their eggs and sanity
Their covert webs of vanity,
Caucuses of secrecy and world control
By the freaky eight legged, arachnids all.
Out of the rabbit hole back home again
Carefully I serve up my curious tale
When back is against shape-shifting wall
Look real hard, you might have a bad fall.
So keep some pills handy Alice, down the rabbit hole
Sometimes you just need to be very, very small
But at other times you might have to be, really very tall.
`twas a great escape and a close call

Fear was the key to escape
But I had to accept the wonder of it all,
How I can be very tall even when I'm small...

*Amrita Valan*

# Unchained Alice

Dream dazzled
Unlocking door
Travelling through
Labyrinthine levels of
Earth-induced euphoria

Solo, so low, slowly
Cheshire Cat grin in the
Crescent Moon again
Unchained Alice, I am.

Escaping reality is an
Artist's very specialty
Down I fall
Fairytale wings
Bells and all

Into the whirlpool spiral
Of the Rabbit hole.

Illusions are favored
By wild-eyed thinkers
Untamed hearts must
Dance and bow to beauty
Craving expression
Sensation
Experience
Height.

Yet it's from rock bottom
That I'll build a castle
Of Questioning
Living as my own

## Down The Rabbit Hole

Imaginative
Unannounced
Queen
Laughing and crying
Mad and inquisitive
Over everything.

*Christa Frazee*

# Ruby Slippers

Emerald city
Monkeys fly in formation
Follow the gold path

*Maggie Mae*

## Mad Hearted Crazy

Lost in a confusion
a labyrinth of haze.
Foggy thoughts obscuring.
Sanity unravels.

Caught up in illusion
the opticals are glazed
inducing lunatic
dreamers to wail quietly.

Chimerically wild minds
playing with delusions.
Happy and ludicrous
demented perfection.

Delicate and crazy
the mad hearted saunter,
in freedom of spirit
and frenzied mania.

*Jacqui Slade*

## The Wizard of Od

Somewhere over the rainbow
Monkeys fly to the Land of Od
Where Dorothy and her cat Tito
have dropped into Munchkin Land.
The munchkin's parade around Dorothy rapping
"Ding dong, the Wicked Warlock is dead!"
During the festivities a giant poof of purple smoke appears.
As it dissipates
Dorothy encounters the Wicked Warlock of the West.
He is intent to possess her ruby high top Converse.
Feeling terrified
Dorothy's braids fly up in the air like Pippy
Longstocking's.
A munchkin blows a huge bubble
that grows and grows 'til suddenly, it pops!
Covered in pink Bazooka Bubble Gum
is Gladwin the Good Warlock of the North.
Waving his sticky wand
he informs the Warlock of the West,
"You have no power here!
Be gone, before somebody drops a trailer on you too!"
Dorothy wearing her fly Converse
and carrying her Star Wars lunchbox
Boogies down the yellow brick road with Tito by her side.
They are on their way to the Sapphire City
to meet The Great and Powerful Od.
During their journey they meet the wise Scarecrow
who needs brain surgery,
The kind Tinman who needs a hip replacement
And the cuddly Cowardly Lion who needs psychotherapy.
The Wicked Warlock is always on their trail.
He hopes the poppies
will make Dorothy and her friends sleep forever

So the ruby Converse will be his.
Gladwin reverses the spell
and instead the poppies make them drunken with laughter.
Arriving in the Sapphire City
Dorothy and her friends are shocked
to see a donkey of a different color.
They are treated to a spa day.
Botox for the Scarecrow
a massage for the Tinman
a pedicure for the cowardly lion,
and a fuchsia dye job for Dorothy.
Holding onto each other nervously
they finally meet the Wizard of Od.
Each one pleading for his help.
He will only grant their wishes
if they bring back the dagger of the Wicked Warlock.
The monkeys fly through the rainbow capturing Dorothy
Bringing her to the Warlock.
He realizes he has to eliminate Dorothy
if he wants those magical ruby high tops.
Dorothy cries out as Tito escapes, "Run Tito, Run!"
While Dorothy weeps and weeps
her friends come to set her free.
However, her tears have created a flowing river
through the corridors of the castle,
Making it hard for a rescue attempt.
The warlock is raging mad
as he starts to disappear into the salty tears.
He screams out, "I'm melting! I'm melting!"
When bringing back the dagger to the Wizard of Od,
Dorothy and her friends realize he is a humbug
but a gentle humbug.
He doesn't have a medical license,

So he refers the Scarecrow, Tinman, and Cowardly Lion
to see the renowned Dr. Seuss.
Suddenly, the Bazooka bubble appears again,
And out pops Gladwin the Good Warlock.
He explains to Dorothy
she always had the power to go back to Las Vegas.
Dorothy clicks her high tops and repeats,
"There's no place like home
there's no place like home."
As Dorothy awakens with Aunt Em by her side,
She mutters "What happens in the Land of Od
stays in the Land of Od."

*Kelly Klein*

Down The Rabbit Hole

Sprinkle magic words upon these

pages poets

## Winky Willy World

Silly Sally saw something strange
While walking wacky in Winky Willy World
Gertrude the goat gliding on a mushroom,
As Flipper Fish flies through the rainbow sky
And a parade of dancing unicorns in glitter outfits going by
My, my, my what a day I should say to laugh and play
Silly Sally begins to yawn
She says, "oh how I wish to stay
But I will be back someday"
as she drifted away in a deep sleep.

*Tammy S. Thomas*

# A Cat's Early Morning Walk

A cat staggered out a house with a pout
For an early morning walk.
He heard the birds yawn as he crossed the lawn
To have a light-hearted talk.
"Morning!" he said to the wakening dew.
(Of course he got no reply.)
Considering the dew, his weight overdue,
He fell, crushing a snail thereby.
The snail!
The snail!
Thinner than the crust of a pie!

Oblivious to the kill the cat went on a hill
To continue his morning walk.
He passed some nice trees and hidden in these
Was a cow who loved to stalk.
Him serenading, her masquerading
As Fate's threads stubbornly spun:
The cat passed her place, the cow picked up pace,
Trailing after the cat for fun!
For fun!
For fun!
Meek, shy, or shameful? She was none!

The cow followed the cat with expertise at that
In want of conversation.
But then she stumbled o'er stones so jumbled
Into the cat - damnation!
Down the hill they rolled as doom did unfold -
They picked up a break-neck speed -
The cat was yelping, the cow not helping
As they neared a huge cliff, indeed!
A cliff!

# Down The Rabbit Hole

A cliff!
The cruel edge of a cliff - oh, heed!

Suddenly!

The cat and the cow stopped rolling somehow
By crashing into a stump.
The cat in a daze was found in a maze
Of cow torso and cow rump.
And slowly the cow did come to just now
To make sense of her surroundings.
Make sense!
Make sense!
Trying to bear her head's poundings!

The cat still hidden, face overridden
With dirt and dirt and more dirt,
Was left all alone, as still as a stone,
As the cow had left to flirt.
(She had spotted some hottie bull with rum
Waiting for her far away….
So off she did run to look for more fun
For the rest of the good, nice day!
Nice day!
Nice day!
An awesome day for much more play!

Thus when the cat came to, no memory nor clue
Had he about what had passed.
He looked at his fur, like that of a cur,
And said, "Fur balls have amassed!"
The cat, so in fear for his coat so dear,
Immediately scampered home.

O'er hills he hurried, past fields he scurried
Into his haven of a home.
His home!
His home!
Into his haven of a home!

*Shawn Chang*

# My Blue Shoes

My blue shoes are like me,
Bright and bubbly as you can see
Keeps me stepping
One, two, three
My blues shoes protects my feet from harm
And they sure do have a lot of charm
My blue shoes are the best no doubt
They make me smile with so much joy
I just want to shout!
My blue shoes,
They keep me looking great in any weather
Those blue shoes...
My hidden treasures

*Tammy S. Thomas*

## A Wish in the Wings

Once a vessel ventured around
from the North into Mildford Sound,
transporting an escaping Prince,
for no passioned plea would evince.
His stepfather, King Tasman ruled
by fear, but his subjects weren't fooled.
Meanwhile, a Fairy blessed the sky
with a touch that could purify;
Te Anau Timaru reigned over
Zealand's forest full of clover.
Through her hypnotic sacred song,
she enticed awe, as time grew long.
Divine dragonflies were entranced,
while bedazzled butterflies danced.
From the Eastern coast they traversed,
flying South as she sang her verse.
Later, they came upon a grove.
There, they would frequent Karmic Kove;
where, in the mists of Fairy Falls,
her fluttering friends, in the thralls,
began to metamorphosize,
changing to fairy-butterflies.
Now, guardians of sanctity,
they preserve the fall's alchemy.
Soon, Prince Tasman had the same view
of falls frolicked by Te Anau.

Then, proceeding beyond, he dove
and swam through that mystical cove,
whereupon, in the still, up stream,
he noticed a reflection's gleam.
Looking up, his enchanted eyes
met Te Anau's with heavy sighs.

Mesmerized, he whispered a wish
to be by her side. Then, vanish!!
In a moment, within their stare,
he was suddenly standing there.
Next, Te Anau slyly exclaimed:
he had two wishes, which remained.
Amazed at this new found surprise,
the proud Prince pondered to be wise.
He could now be King, yet instead,
wished Te Anau and he would wed.
With this second wish granted
Te Anau coyishly canted:
A dutiful wife she would be,
but her whole heart did not agree.
With one wish left, he was spellbound
as he chose heart over the crown.
Unaware that he was beguiled,
Te Anau engagingly smiled,
for unbeknownst to him was fated;
A wish in the wings still waited.

*Justin R. Hart*

# The Circus

They said my cousin
 ran away with the circus.
He quoted,
"Mum, I've had enough,
So I'm going to go
 play with the lions."

I on the other hand
would rather believe he ran away to be a star.
Sometimes I was the only one
who knew how caged up he had felt.
It made sense that he had
wanted to be in the spotlight.

They said my cousin ran away with the circus.
What fun to see all of the beautiful colors,
elegance and challenge of the fine acrobats!

My mum once said,
"It's just one big happy freak show!
Only one out of their right mind
would want to join the circus!"

I applauded my cousin.
It was about time someone was smart enough
to leave this bland of a small town.

Too many lawyers...
too many police...
Too much gossip.
Others go to bed -
while some may not even sleep!

My cousin ran away with the circus...
How I wish I had his heart and courage
to follow a wild and crazy dream!

My mum said,
"Now don't you be
thinking anything weird!
You certainly don't want
to grow up to be like your cousin!"

So I thought to myself
No- I certainly don't.

Last night, I ran away
to be with the gypsies.
They all say my cousin
is back from the circus.
I heard he was a star.

*Ariana R. Cherry*

# Wander Land

Heart skips and race
Mind trying to keep pace
Don't fall apart
Before you start
Take five giant steps towards
Sanity with curious words
Control your serious soul
In this lovely rabbit hole.

*Shelly Ambrose*

# Wakeful Dreaming

Untether imagination's secret bog
ease the mind into a pleasant fog
escaping within eyes at half-mast
toward stories from childhood past.
Travel upon the bricks of yellow
laughing with a lion so mellow
soar with Pan and battle Hook
if it gets too scary close the book.
No need to drag the friends along
don't worry if you forgot the song.
When you encounter mighty Kong
rabbit will always share his bong.
And if perchance you meet a cat
who's head's adorned with many hats
he may offer green eggs and spam
check the spyware for Sam I am.
Should you see a blue giraffe
it's just forgotten how to laugh.
Give to him a hug that's mellow
I'm sure he will turn back to yellow.
On those days when feeling old
ride a rainbow to the pot of gold
and whether you're a boy or girl
go with Sparrow to sail the Pearl.
Gobble chocolate with a boy named Willy
although the thought of it might feel silly.
Remember why these stories fill your head
to chase away those thoughts you dread.

*Valormore De Plume*

# Peter Pan

With mischievous
thoughts on his mind
he soars high
above the wind
playing a chord
on his flute
he refuses to age
into youth
his never ending adventures
in Neverland
sometimes to the outside world
it also expands
with fairies and pirates
on the mystical island
his contact peaceful
sometimes violent
as leader of the lost boys
his flute makes a dominant noise

*Bevan Boggenpoel*

## Shades of Orange

Waking up in the district of Torridge
Time to put some orange
On the top of my porridge
So my body is getting some storage
I passed on bacon and sausage
Because in my fridge was a shortage
Trying something new takes courage
Going to take a ride up to Norwich
The birds are singing out in coral
Kamakaze cat thinks he is immortal
Looking at the plants that are floral
I waved to my neighbour Laurel
Who was smiling having a chortle
Get my sweater on so I am warming
Looking out the sky is a nice shade of orange

*Steve Lay*

# Wonderland

I'm closing my eyes
Gonna count up to three
Then I'll flip on the switch
To an alternate me
Whirling and twirling
A bit out of control
Lickity split
Down the rabbit hole
Fusion, confusion
I'm still spinning around
Another flip of the switch
I land face flat on the ground
Fumbling, stumbling
I reach for a door
Trip over my feet
As I step through the floor
The tassels are hassles
When ringing the bell
It leaves me to wonder
Where I actually fell
But happy I am
By the touch of a hand
Let the magic begin
It's Wonderland

*Lyne Beringer*

## Shhh! I'm Catching a Buzz!

I watched the rabbit slip through the gate
into the private garden of my neighbor's
prized pot plants.

My neighbor had complained that rabbits
must be getting in and feasting on his
fabulous foliage.

I stealthily approached hoping to catch
this larcenous leporid in the act. And there he was,
chewing on a leaf or two, not even noticing me.

I took another step, a twig cracked, the rabbit
looked up and saw me.
For what seemed like an eternity, both of us
were frozen, transfixed and staring at each other.

Then the rabbit stood up on his hind legs
and started a bunny boogie break dance
performing a rendition of the rabbit robot
morphing into the moon walk and then
a split, into a head spin.

He stood up again, pointed at me with his
front paw, gave a sly wink and disappeared
in a mad flash dash into the bushes

That hare was high on hemp, a real Buzz Bunny.
I wonder if he had known that the plants
were grown from seeds of medical marijuana
would he have asked, "Wazzup Doc?"

*Peter V. Dugan*

Taste the adventure that awaits

## Rainbow Slide

I was chillin up on a puffy cloud
All laid back feeling kinda proud
When I heard some partiers getting loud
They looked like a pretty cool crowd

So I slid all the way down the rainbow
But I slid so fast my hiney was all aglow
I reckon it was quite a dandy aftershow
But I couldn't see it, so I wouldn't know

My blue jeans were now scorched
My buttock were completely torched
I'd always wanted a nice brown tan
But right now I prefer a cooling fan

Tried to sit down at the table to eat
But my tushy was emanating too much heat
My tummy was empty and in a bind
But my main concern was my burning behind

I ran and cannonballed into the pool
Oh so thankful for the instant cool
Think I'll leave rainbows alone for a while
And that decision made my booty smile!

*D.B. Hall*

## Milk Chocolate Meltdown

Oh
If this place we're made of chocolate
I'd be homeless
It's true
I'd eat this tiny house down to the ground
Maybe even the grass too
Sure
I would probably feel a little sickly
But who can resist
The creamy twist
Of a milk chocolate tree in the backyard!

*Elizabeth Daniel*

## Mythical Magic

Filled with fantasy
and discovery
Imagination just
running free
The impossible
made possible
Adventure
unstoppable
Jaw dropping scenes
taking you places
you've never seen
or ever been
Flying through the sky
emotional scenes
makes you want to cry
Magic and artistry
locked up in mystery
Mythical islands filled with
fairies and mermaids
Taking you on a
unbelievable crusade
A place where you
never grow old
Where villains are weak
and heroes are bold

*Bevan Boggenpoel*

## Chasing Rainbows While Stuck on Narcotics (Prescription of course!)

Chasing after endless arches of rainbows
I spotted a little strange fairy elf
who was looking for silver
I asked him if he knew
where the pot of gold was
but he told me it had went down in value.

My mind couldn't comprehend
why he would be
at the end of the rainbow
when gold wasn't his goal.
Perhaps silver is the next big thing?

Under the promising rainbow,
I saw a multi-dimensional world
with rows of lime green pink trees,
and soft beds of grass that were
as blue as the earthly sky
or maybe the sky was down
on the ground
And I was standing on the clouds?

My mind couldn't comprehend how I got
to this other worldly rainbow land
on my search for gold
but now, the little fairy elf told me,
that I would be better off with silver
and for some reason,
a song of silver and gold
rang in my ears.

## Down The Rabbit Hole

Here I stood, befuddled and stuck in
this fantasy rainbow land
where the passing clouds
were a fluffy purple
and the warm blinding sunshine
splashed my face, literally.

I tried to comprehend
the battle of silver and gold.
But was that the truth
that I needed to focus on?
Or was it that I needed
to find the end of the rainbow?

I looked above to the inquisitive
stars for my baffling answers
their flashes of gold light
streaked across the
dark nighttime sky.

Little bulbs of brightness,
all glimmering to the same merry dance tune.
Could they answer the questions
that lay heavy on
my wandering mind?
Twas it gold or silver
or was there another impossible truth to find?

*Ariana R. Cherry*

## Haunted Solstice

Just before you doze off to sleep
you hear them outside the window
in the garden on a hot summer night.
A band of nomadic gnomes known
as the Yellowbelly Scuttlebutts.
True musical morticians who play
the razzmatazz jazz of real hepcat
banjoists and hipster harmonicas.

Dressed in their trademark off-color
chinchilla jackets, iridescent nightwear,
and Raman-noodle loafers, they
intermingle the newest passion of fashion

With their makeshift inversions
of discordant notes, that taunt and tease
the frenzy of scattered words, a fast shuffle
of changing phases and turning phrases.

A cacophony of mixed melodies
evoke a sense of remorse and revved-up
rebuke, as rows daffodils evaporate in
the light of the electrified moonshine.

Amid ghosts of the aroused void,
new and frighteningly deformed creatures,
monsters, spawned by imagination
and fears, crawl out from the muck
of one's mind to bask in the shadows cast
by the mist that shrouds the haloed moon.
There will be no sleep tonight.

*Peter V. Dugan*

# Dorothy

Spiraling through dreams, hurricanes of mind
searching for something that you cannot find.
In wistful tornadoes a wish is blown
over the rainbow, you find yourself thrown.
Living in colour avenging the grey
in wonder wayfarer finding your way
through perils and sadness your journey starts
hoping you'll find the home of your heart.

With each step you take your shoes glitter red
each sparkle a mirror of light in your head.
Your pace small in stature, but huge in stride.
Which way you go is for you to decide.
Melodramatic your faith in your charm.
Conscience will guide you, protect you from harm.
Tempted by fields of malevolent guise
perfumed to trick but awakened you're wise.

Your path is golden, tenacious your soul
to battle your demons you have control.
In cinematic musical aplomb
you start to realize how far you have come.
Resolute not to stray in your motion
you find there is no magic or potion.
The magician you seek lives in your thoughts
you have the answers to all you have sought.

Prowess unleashes the lion and you
find courage and roar pride in your truth.
Your head wasn't filled with bales of straw
intelligent, wise of that you are sure.
Your heart not leaden with grief but with love
you come through stronger the journey's been rough.

The home of your heart is where your love lies
no grasses greener and no bluest skies.

*Jacqui Slade*

## A Little Wicked

Last night a Munchkin,
today she sits alone again
in the sandbox.

Dorothy, home from Oz,
thumps her red sneakers together.
Says, "Look, look, look!"
and sings, "I see Paris, I see France.
Let's put sand in her underpants."
She pulls and stretches
the Munchkin's elastic waistband .

The Lion, afraid to protest, watches.
The heartless Tin Woodsman gawks,
and the Scarecrow, too, stands by.

Dorothy's aunty petitions the principal,
as though she's The Wizard,
to no avail.

And that's how Dorothy
gets suspended and
misses the cast party.

*Mary Langer Thompson*

# Rabbit Hole Poets

If you don't know where you're going
any road will do
yellow bricks, approaching madness
floorboards and flattops
play it like you mean it.

Music leaps from hot, metal bridges
never leaving a note
dragged down the rabbit hole
with mushrooms and sages
crumbs of art hung on cobwebs
gobbled up by ravens
collecting shiny things.

Tangled balls of verbs and yarn
words weaving phrases
write it like you mean it.

Creativity, the sweetest addiction
junkies to the word, the melody
take me away, to that silly place
where rational walks a tightrope
rabbit hole poets, ravens tapping
collecting shiny things
write like a madman.

Words can't kill, they'll cut you bad
art leaves a scar
bleed me like you mean it.

*Hugh Dysart*

## I Am Woman!

I am woman! They proudly declare
I thought I would try it but lacked the flair.
As soon as I said it, a man popped out of thin air
From the Ministry of We'll Make You Despair.

I'm sorry he said but you don't qualify
So the statement you made, we suspect, is a lie.
But it says it on my Certificate of Birth!
And on my passport, for what it's worth.

He took out his clipboard, he clicked his pen
Cleared his throat with a polite 'ahem'
Jewelry, he said, fails to delight
And, right now, you look a fright!
Flat shoes and trousers and big comfy tops!
And when was the last time you shopped 'til you dropped?
You don't wear make-up or dress to impress
Frankly my dear, you look quite a mess.
You never diet or worry about weight
You'd better shape up before it's too late.

His remarks were really beginning to rankle
As my walking stick went straight for his ankle.

You can't deny it, you batty old bat!
You never, EVER eat chocolate!
We can't register you as 'man' - you lack the parts.
But as a 'woman' - you lack the arts.

I was handed a chit
Which classified me 'IT' - GIT!

*Susan E Birch*

## Dorothy's Discovery

She was a summer storm of slate grey and hot breezes shifting through the fields of poppies straight in the path of the twister. Her ruby red dress fell about her hips like a hot late evening sunset.

Calm and serene she accepted her fate, to collide with that twister, each step through the sea of red making her eyes heavy and heart light. The winds whipped through the meadow and still she kept moving forward toward her undoing.

The turbulence struck her like so many pent up fears as she found herself swept away by the storm. Still she remained peaceful, sleepy eyed and dreaming of clearer skies.

It was then that she found herself inside the vortex, no more howling winds or slate grey clouds. She looked up and saw bright blue sky and flashes of lightning through the whirlwind. Now she understood it was never the bluster that mattered, but the peace she could find within the storm.

*Tracy Seiden*

## Cabbage Dreams

I am dreaming my cabbage dream.
I'm peeling off the outer leaves
to find what lies hidden beneath.
Looks much the same as the outer leaf
a little less battered and crinkled
but fundamentally the same.
Now for the next layer
There's a drop of water
shining full of light
and something darker, more solid
the leavings of some hidden creature.
Another layer reveals the holes
and the sleepy caterpillar
dreaming
without his pipe
without his crown,
so unsure of
his own
identity
much less mine.
If I peel off
layer after layer until
I get to the heart of it,
will I understand where I've come from
and be able to unpack the dream,
find the pipe and put the pieces
together, make sense of the
cabbage, crown the king.

*Lynn White*

*First published in Poetry Breakfast, June 11, 2016*

Let your words dance along golden pathways

# Playing With Kings

I had a vision of kings that went as it will go
standing around a pyre dancing to and fro.
In my mind these kings they sang
they sang the songs of old
they made a jolly party and frolicked oh, oh.
These kings they did not sit on thrones
no scepters did they hold.
These kings had no subjects and no lands
 but they were oh so bold.
These kings were simple people
who danced and skipped and played
they showed all the rest of us what ruling was
and gladly we obeyed.
When it came right down to it
these kings for us
would bleed
it was only right for us to pay homage
and to them heed.
If you came upon them
I know just what you would say
"can I join you oh king
can I come and with you and play,"
these kings were jolly people
and they liked a good old time
they would invite you into their circle
and ask of you a rhyme.
Give to them the words I say
give them true and true
don't worry about the cadence
just make sure the words are from you.
Keep them simple, keep them short
or make them hugely long,
but to please these kings

you must ensure that these words are yours
and not borrowed wrong
When you come to see these kings for what they really are
you will be more reverent at their dancing pyre.
As the flames lick into the sky
these kings they dance and fly
they sing and ask of you
to only bring your heart, so they do.
So keep in mind that when I saw those kings that day
that I went into their circle
and I danced and danced the very night away.
When I awoke the kings were gone
but on the ground was a winter song
written in a time just before the dawn.
On the bottom clear as day
these kings they certainly had their say
because they put there for all to see
the words that are with me to so very sincerely.
In the kings script they stated clear
that in order to come back I must be ever sincere
they noted not once but twice in a row
that I was to keep the flame burning
or peril I would know.
Not a threat but a warning
I would say to keep my heart open
and share it each day.
I built up the fire and continued to dance
knowing that in time my kings they would be back
I opened my heart and saw in many ways
that the pyre grew higher and higher each day.
Keep the faith!

*Dale E. Werner*

## Punctuality is the Key

Late
Late
Late
Look at the time
Always behind
Schedules don't keep themselves you know
Pour a cup of tea nervously
Throw it back
Oh who has the time?
My list
Where is my list?
Under my hat I see
I'll tip it as I'm scurrying by
In a flurry!
Top of the morning to ye'
Late
Late
Late
Rarely
Hardly ever
Almost never
On time.

*Elizabeth Daniel*

## Sleepy Beauty

Life is an unbalanced beam
When I forget to daydream.
I close my eyes
See peace in disguise
Dancing out of a colorful steam
As my favorite flavor ice cream.
I take a bite, and it seems
I'm swimming in streams of glitter
Where worries whither
And villains can't scheme
All is agleam.
Gliding through shine
Souls rest and recline.
Then a sudden buzz and screech
I lose control of my speech.
Laughing in twirl and swirl
I open my eyes and hurl
Toward a screaming alarm
That I unplug with no harm.
"Now, not another peep
I'm going back to sleep!"

*Shelly Ambrose*

## Neverland

"I do not believe in fairytales."
Said the man wandering Neverland
scavenging for his youth.
Take some advice from me lad
you will not like how this story ends.
You will come to see as enticing
as pixies may be they bore easily.
You will never keep pace
with the lost boys who overdose
on desire daily.
Once time is lost
it is never to be found.
But who am I to tell such tales
I'm just a man with a hook for a hand.

*Kristi L. Phillips*

# Rabbit Hole

This way or that way
there is only one way
you must flee!
Oh the Doctors, the Doctors
you must see!
You're mad, mad
mad as the Hatter
Your life disarray!
Take this pill, take that pill
tame the dismay!
Chasing White Rabbits
with pretty pastels
locking your emotions
away in cells.
Cheshires will vanish,
do not dwell.
You will be safe, safe
safe from this Hell!
Demeaning voices
the Queen that I dread.
denying her role in the
damage which has been bred.
With my silence I scream
Off With Her Head!
Ravens and writing desks
house mice and tea
I'll do what is best, best
best for me.
Through the looking glass
I shall proceed
wandering, wandering
I shall be free.
If Alice was the only one so bold

# Down The Rabbit Hole

to fall down the rabbit hole
there would be very few stories
ever to be told.

*Kristi L. Phillips*

## Like Alice

I'm too big
I'm too small
I can't I fit in
fit into this, rabbit hole world
any more than I did the other
the above ground world
Both can't be wrong
can they?
It must be me
that doesn't fit
that can't be made
to fit into them
Me that's wrong.

Both worlds can't be wrong
can they?

*Lynn White*

*First published in Poetry Breakfast, September 2016*

## Home Sweet Home

Begging troubles to melt
Like sticky lemon drops
Itching to soar wild and free
Scanning the sky for
Rainbow-wrapped Twisters
Hoping, like a bird
One might carry me
For I have every intention of
Finding my brave song
My purpose here is
To seek, to speak
To reach a point of
Peaceful passion
Perhaps a sublimely
Undemanding type of
Personal understanding.
The old Black and White
Wounds bleed in with a
Truer technicolor
Insisting on
Sparkling
Ruby steps
Upon Time's
Golden road
I will die still
Holding onto the
Brightest spectrum
Of Innocent Hope
Forever scrambling to
Utilize the Brain
Pleading to speak
Aloud with Heart
Crying for Courage in

## Down The Rabbit Hole

The thickness of every
Bewildered wilderness
The adventure
The journey
The roads all
Lead me to this
Inner destination
Finally felt within
As Home sweet Home

*Christa Frazee*

# Ruby Slippers

All she ever wanted
Was a pair of ruby slippers
The sparkle and glimmer
Of the red so hypnotic

Her green skin
Her cackling laugh
Always left out
Of her sisters games

If only she had
Those pretty red slippers
The boys wouldn't notice
How unpleasant she looks

They would be
Mesmerized by those
Magical sparkling ruby slippers
Maybe giving her a first kiss

*Maggie Mae*

## You Are Mad Dear Grandma

"You are mad dear Grandma" the young man opined
"And my friends all think you're a fright
Your thoughts are often insanely inclined
And your fancy too often takes flight!"

"When I was young" his Grandma replied
"I was constantly kept in my place
Now that I'm older and wiser beside
I am pleased to opt out of the race."

"You're a Looney dear Grandma," (his voice quite chill)
"When you threaten to bury our bones
Then say that you won't dig us up until
You feel we have properly atoned."

"As a child," said his Gran "I was constantly told
To be seen but never to be heard.
So now I am pleased to be allowed to be bold
And make statements outrageously absurd."
"You are crazy dearest Gran" he said with a grin
"And possibly seriously deranged.
I don't think, in this argument, I'm going to win
But I'd hate it if you happened to change."
"Dear boy," said his Grandma, "You've said quite enough
And that smile almost makes my heart break.
Come sit down beside me and we'll chat about stuff.
If you're good I will knit you a cake!"


*Susan E Birch*


*Inspired by 'You are old Father William' by Lewis Carroll*

## Larry and the Fly

Larry the frog was hopping
along looking for breakfast
When he heard a cry
It was a fly stuck in a web
What a wonderful surprise,
Larry exclaimed as he licked his lips and ready for his treat.

The spider crept up behind him
And said, "oh how sweet, fresh meat
you will make my meal complete".
As the spider shoots his web to capture Larry,

He jumps back and lets his tongue out to attack
And caught the spider with one smack and down the hatch
he goes.

The fly was happy and says my hero.
But little do he know he was next
Larry turns around and starts to stare
and the fly says, "oh please you wouldn't dare"!

Larry laughs and says, "who will save you now"?
As he hops over and let his tongue out again
misses the fly and broke the web
and was stuck with his tongue wrapped around a tree

The fly was broke free
And as he flew by and laughed, he says to the frog,
"Thank you for saving me".

*Tammy S. Thomas*

# Harvey

The friendly dog sits inside
Waiting for it to be bright
It's raining cats and maybe dogs
Maybe even toads and frogs
All he wants is to go out and play
But maybe he will have to wait for a sunny day

The friendly dog hears the noise
From outside while he chews his toys
But how many times can he lick his bone
Before he gets bored and roams
His family sees this they love and care
Some sunshine they want to share.

The friendly dog sits inside
There he sat he looked outside and saw a cat
The cat hissed and the dog growled
He was jealous of the cat who had just sat
Under some trees, as the wind and the breeze
As those beautiful chocolate eyes looked and fantasized

The friendly dog lay in his bed
His ears were always pricking at what was said
Suddenly he awoke from his sleep
There was something lighter that he could see
The rain had stopped it was dry outside
He no longer had to stay in and hide

He was looking forward to letting loose
On a wet garden that for a few days was not used
Just like that it was time to go out
His tail started wagging he was barking out loud
The door flung open as he sprung from his bed

# Down The Rabbit Hole

He flew down the garden without even being fed

The friendly dog who for a few days sat inside
Flew down the garden without being fed
Nearly knocked himself in the head
He was so excited, the spring in his step
As he jumped around the garden making a mess
The friendly dog was free to play
In a garden he loves still to this day

*Steve Lay*

A place where words achieve goals

created by dreams

## A Ghostly Cold
## (Ode to the Flying Dutchman)

"Hark!" they cry, "come here and soon"
Under a darkening sky and palest moon
We spy a ship, adrift in the bay
her sails wrapped tight, empty helm I'd say
She slows to a stop and the anchor falls
The Tower sounds an alarm, come one and all
The Colonel hollers, "Make yourself known!"
but all we hear are creaks, moans, and groans
Longboats, soldiers muskets, swords and such
A comical sight to behold, I found a bit too much
It's quiet and empty on her dampened deck
So clean and pristine, she's hardly a wreck
We row back to shore and toss out the hook
Unsettled and wet, we turn round and look
She's gone! all scream; that legend of old
Twas the Flying Dutchman I'm sure
a true Ghostly Cold

*Ken Allan Dronsfield*

# Wonderland

A little bite of this
A tiny sip of that
Only time will see
What will become of me
Taller, taller still
Smaller, smaller til
I can fit through the door
Just a little bit more
What adventure awaits
If only I find the key

Tick tock tick tock
The clickity clack of the clock
Time for tea
Tea time tea time
No time for tea
Tick tock tick tock
Off to chase the clock
The white rabbit
Is off to see
What time is tea?

Off, off with his head
Red is all I see
Why, why can't they
Just agree with me
Off, off with her head
She just doesn't see
How wonderful it can be
Living here with me

So sad, so mad
The Hatter is to see

## Down The Rabbit Hole

Cannot find his ribbons
Because he only has eyes for thee
Buttons, bows and ribbons
All over the floor
If the hats not ready by four
His head will hit the floor
So sad, so mad
The Hatter must be
Trapped in a land
Only I can see

*Maggie Mae*

# From One Cirrus to Another

What do you suppose the clouds talk about?
"Lovely weather we're having today!"
"I feel a slight chance of rain coming on"
"Should we warn them down there with a little thunder?"
"Perhaps we should hold our breath and be a bit darker"
"Nah, we'll just let them be surprised
I hear that one over there loves rain"
"Let's give her a downpour!"
See this is what I imagine they say to one another
As I'm watching them float idly by
Wondering
Are they just as curious about me?

*Elizabeth Daniel*

## Alice in Wonderland

Staring about
she saw a rabbit
she followed it
a curiosity habit
she climbed down
the rabbit hole
but falls a long way
to a curious hall
she finds many doors
locked on her paths
she also meets
the queen of hearts
the attractive garden
filled with adventure
looks like a play land
filled with pleasure
she finds herself
deep underground
where different characters
on her way is found
It's a myriad of fantasy
doubting if
she wants to break free
excitement and rivalry
that she meets
some friend's carnations
others weeds
Alice in Wonderland
full of discovery
her journeys can be cruel
but yet so lovely

*Bevan Boggenpoel*

# Enchantment

Mirror, Mirror crooked on my wall
Sparkling for all to see
You make my ego stand twelve feet tall
With the strength of Twenty –three
Reflections refuse to tell one flaw
Youth is your eternal guarantee
As I hear you call
"Fairest of all you'll forever be."

*Shelly Ambrose*

## Open Season

Animals
hated him
He felt sure
Now he was convinced

Crossing
the campus
notebook in hand
he spotted the goose

Geese
seem to
make honking sounds
This one barked loudly

Following
behind him
a quickened pace
honking in hot pursuit

Huge
running goose
feathers flapping furiously
increased speed, catching up

Goose
behind him,
honking, barking, angry
Biting his right buttock

Animals
hated him
He felt sure

Now he was convinced.

*Brenda-Lee Ranta*

# Autumn's Ascending Spring

At Fall's finish, when darkness surged stronger
Autumn's sprite lamented, looking longer
into the specks of gold, gleaming to see
within the eyes of the wise wizardtree
whom, with just one wave of his branch to raise
transformed each charmed leaf to mirror his gaze.
The hue of his eyes harmonized the eves
as season's spectrum transposed from his leaves
to real eyes Autumn was mesmerized
possessed by enchantment and hypnotized
by one wink of their glistening glitter.
Fall's fairy filled of golden leaf litter
when Winter approached and tried to take hold
Autumn just wouldn't let go of the gold
Winter could not turn over a new leaf
without first taking on a new belief.
He must become a scrounging sneak, so sly
poaching from this sordid season's Shanghai
swiftly swindling a heist in his gambit
to now become an embezzling bandit.
So, he secretly stole and forged ahead,
retrieving his yearly pickings and fled
in his larceny of lifting leaves gleam,
faded from such an enriched color scheme;
and so, he tried to collect all the gold,
whence Winter would witness Fall's final fold.
She couldn't compete with wily Winter
who implicated, at season's splinter
an oblivious breeze, that blindly blew
caught in a kleptomania taboo
rustling and prowling with the thief of Time
cohorts consorting in their daze of crime.
As wayward Winter sheared Autumn's suture

she tried to take the Fall into the future.
Yet, her presence was past to the leaf thieves
just when Winter took all his gold 'n leaves.

Whence Winter took all of his gold 'n leaves,
he would begin to freeze the landscapes' eves
with seasonal diamonds dusting the earth
trimming the trees, crystallizing their worth.
Yet, Wizardtree's burdened branches bowed
in hibernation, they carried the load.
He dreamt of his recently departed
as Autumn was dormant when it started.
While Winter wiled in ornamental ice
Spring's sprite soon slipped in to hide her veiled vice.
Quickly, she spotted the glistening gems
upon the quiescent Wizardtree's stems.
Spring plucked the crystals into her basket
which was covered by cloth, just to mask it.
With each crystal lifted, Wizardtree stirred.
His eyes opened, yet still there was no word.
In the midst of playing with his jewels
Winter was aroused by sprouting toadstools.
Then, he spotted Spring stealing his treasure
as she gazed at Wizardtree with pleasure
 so, with the aid of his accomplice, Gale
winds blew, bellowing blows frosted with hale.
Her tempestuous tempest tumbled Spring,
sent back to the future for seasoning.
Now, Winter possessed her basket in hand,
before it became only contraband.
For when he reached for his precious jewels,
he found his gems had melted into pools.
Left with his own reflection staring back

his time had passed for the vernal hi-jack.
Meanwhile, the ruckus of the supposed heist
awoke Wizardtree and had him enticed.
He stretched to break from his shackles of frost
shaking off Winter would be what was lost.
Swiftly, Spring took this chance to bounce back in
Just before the day began to blacken.
Winter flurried in with one last attempt
yet, failed, as shown by his sudden contempt
as Spring stood between to shield Wizardtree
while Winter's fleeting flakes ended his spree.
Next, snowdrift swayed clear of her heated breath
falling to her extended hand towards death
because her warmth could wilt each frozen rime
through her fingers, water would drop in time
melting from the warmth of her ascent
that held perfection but for a moment
changing like diamonds transformed back to coal,
fueling Spring's embryonic seeded soul.

*Justin R. Hart*

# Kitty Kisses

Fluffy, curly-headed, looney ball!
He jumps upward and bounces off the walls.
Thwack! (Kerplunk)
Then he curls up, snoring in his sleep.
(Huuuuuuuhh. guhrrrrrrr huuuu grrrr
grrrgrrr…..siiiiiiiiiiiiiiiiiiiiiiiiiiiiiiiiiiiiii…)
He is such a such a noble cat!
Sometimes I call him Gerard Erickson.
Sometimes I call him Sanders Pennington.
He speaks, cat, dog, human:
"Tomcat, are you going to eat the dog's leg, perhaps?"
(rub, rub, up-tail)
"Sspurr –ior! But.. I would paw – fer beef steak."
(Huuuuuuuhh. guhrrrrrrr huuuu grrrrr)
"Are the chicken wings too bad for you?"
(blglglblglllgbbblglblgllbgglgllghghghghh)
A roasted mouse in the microwave?
"Disa-purr-!, slave!"
(P – KIIIIIIIIIHHHHHHHHHHHH!!!)
Before that, scratch my elevator – butt!
Then he turns, in Dead Mousie pose, and clumsily
mumbles orders:
"Open My door"
"Close My Window"
"No, do some "Prairie-Doggin'"!
"Do some Cat – Dance!"
Both left feet moving
Then
Both right feet moving
"Walk like a cat, you, clumsy camel!
Think like a cat!
More kitty – like! That's it.
More kitty – like.

More more cattitude!
You have no style, let's get you to ballet!"
He sings soprano (Mrrrowwww. Mrrowwww.
mrrrrrowwwww.)
"Merry Meow Birthday, my Batler, where are you?
Happy Meow, too you, too!
Fetch me my slippers!
Pass on my reading glasses!
I have to get my higher degree.
Heeeeeeere kittykitttykittikitttykitty!
Heeeeeeere kittykitttykittikitttykitty!
Heeeeeeere kittykitttykittikitttykitty!
Go kitty! …Off"
Winding Up
Digging In
Revving Up
Once he is in his cat – cradle
I am telling him tales to his fluffy tail
He is my, fur real, Claw-some friend
He is my dearest and purrrr-fect son
Arm to paw
Cheek to cheek
Heart to heart
Lips to muzzle (mwahhhh)
(Lub-dub…lubdub….lub-dub… Lubdub….)

*Leila Samarrai*

# Walk the Walk

She ran by me
Startled, I said, MMMPH!
She stopped
She turned around
She came back
She looked at me
"You were saying something?"
No
I mean
I have a cat now
This is a whole different ball game
You've been here before, haven't you?
You must have
Either that or you're very sociable
But I have a cat
"Your cat doesn't scare me!"
You don't know my cat. She scares ME!
"It's all in the attitude."
I hope you know what you're doing
"Walk the walk," she said, and scurried away


*Maria Barba*

## Unrestrained Dreams

When you drift off to sleep in your bed
Visions of magical things in your head
Maybe Peter Pan slips in your window
And away, away to Neverland you'll go

Be careful there if you hear a tick of a clock
You will know there approaches giant croc
Who once had Captain Hook in quite a bind
Bit off Hook's hand, and almost his behind

He's always hungry and ferocious as can be
Always wanting to eat a lost boy or three
And he'd really love to snack on daring Peter Pan
He's not satisfied with just his ol nasty Hook's hand

From the murky deep this ferocious beast prowls
A tick tock warning his belly will always growl
Let me warn you before Tinkerbell sprinkles her dust
That croc's sly smile is one you cannot trust

Not every dream is a dream some are an adventure
Make sure you are ready before you go… make sure
Some don't make it back and some return changed
But would you go for the chance to live unrestrained

*D.B. Hall*

# Epilogue

# Publishing Assistance

Starving Artist

In 2013 Ms. Raja Williams realized that there was a gap, a void if you will, within the publishing industry. A writer either had to come up with hundreds, sometimes thousands of dollars to release a book or take on the journey of self-publishing alone. There was no middle ground, no one there to assist, either financially or lead the way in self-publishing. Most writers do not have the finances to pay a publisher, and some don't know where to start when it comes to self-publishing, nor are they prepared to be in business for themselves.

Raja was inspired to start a fund to assist writers in becoming published authors at either a discounted rate or a full publishing scholarship. To begin this fund Raja paid for the publishing of our first anthology Love, a Four Letter Word. Comprised of poets from all around the world. The sales generated from the purchases of the book were placed into a fund that enabled us to fund future publishings.

We now are able to offer anthology publications, a chance for authors to have a voice in the literary world yearly, and we have been able to offer several authors full scholarships, as well as offering deeply discounted publishing services as a whole. We are thankful for the continued support of this program by both our readers and writers alike.

**For More Information Please Visit Our Website At:**

www.ctupublishinggroup.com/starving-artist-fund.html

# Creative Talents Unleashed

## Get Connected With Us!

**Website:** Creative Talents Unleashed Publishing Group

www.ctupublishinggroup.com

**Facebook**: Get connected with us on our Facebook Page

www.Facebook.com/Creativetalentsunleashed

**Twitter:** https://twitter.com/CTUPublishing

**Blog:** www.creativetalentunleashed.com

**Pinterest:** https://www.pinterest.com/creativetalents/

**Instagram:** https://instagram.com/ctupublishinggroup/

# Creative Talents Unleashed

Creative Talents Unleashed is an independent publishing group that offers writers an opportunity to share their writing talents with the world. We are committed to fostering and honoring the work of writers of all cultures. Our publishing group offers writing tips to assist writers in continued growth and learning, daily writing prompts and challenges to keep the writers mind sharp and challenged, marketing and events, as well as a variety of yearly publishing opportunities. We are honored to be assisting writers in the journey of becoming published authors.

www.ctupublishinggroup.com

**For More Information Contact:**

Creativetalentsunleashed@aol.com

www.ingramcontent.com/pod-product-compliance
Lightning Source LLC
Chambersburg PA
CBHW071312060426
42444CB00034B/1972